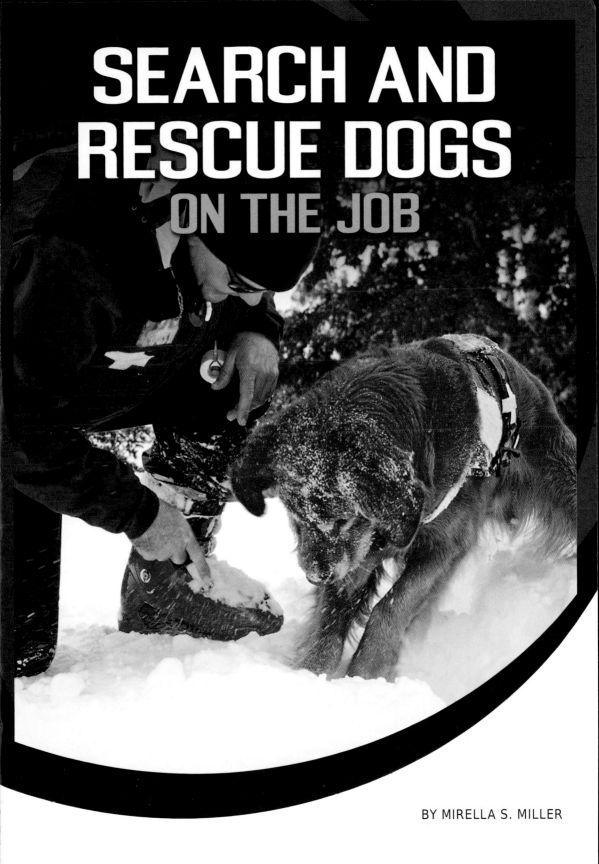

SEARCH AND RESCUE DOGS
ON THE JOB

BY MIRELLA S. MILLER

The Child's World®
childsworld.com

Published by The Child's World®
1980 Lookout Drive • Mankato, MN 56003-1705
800-599-READ • www.childsworld.com

Photographs ©: Figure8Photos/iStockphoto, cover, 1; Andrea Booher/FEMA News Photo, 5; Shutterstock Images, 6, 10, 20; Jessica Lea/UK Department for International Development, 8; Kyodo Extra/AP Images, 9; Marcella Miriello/Shutterstock Images, 12; Sgt. John Crosby, 14; Stoyan Yotov/Shutterstock Images, 15; Kim Raff/The News & Advance/AP Images, 16; Degtyaryov Andrey/Shutterstock Images, 17; US Agency for International Development, 18

ISBN 9781503816152

LCCN 2016945654

Printed in the United States of America
PA02318

TABLE OF CONTENTS

FAST FACTS

The Job

- Search and rescue (SAR) dogs use their senses of smell to find missing people. They work with human **handlers**.

- SAR dogs might be needed after a natural disaster, such as an earthquake or a hurricane. Other times, SAR dogs are used to help find children or adults who are lost.

Training Time

- It can take between two and three years before a search dog is ready to join an official search and rescue team.

- Dogs and their handlers train up to three times each week.

Common Breeds

- Belgian Malinois
- Bloodhound
- Border collie
- German shepherd
- Golden retriever
- Labrador retriever

Famous Dogs

- Barry was a Saint Bernard that lived in the early 1800s. He was a rescue dog in the mountains of Switzerland. He saved more than 40 people's lives.

- Jake was a Labrador retriever that responded to the scene of the September 11, 2001, terrorist attacks. He also worked as a rescue dog after Hurricane Katrina and Hurricane Rita.

- Appollo was a German shepherd that worked with the New York City Police Department. He was the first SAR dog to look for survivors after the September 11 attacks.

Chapter 1

SEARCHING THE RUBBLE

O n April 25, 2015, a 7.8 **magnitude** earthquake rocked the country of Nepal. Buildings in the capital city and surrounding areas crumbled. Thousands of people were missing. They were trapped in the **rubble** caused by the earthquake. These people needed to be saved quickly.

Rescue teams arrived to look for the missing people. Six U.S. search and rescue (SAR) dogs and their handlers flew to Nepal to help. One of these teams included Stetson and his handler, Andy Olvera.

Stetson and Olvera climbed over the rubble. It was not a safe area. Concrete and other materials shifted unexpectedly. But the team was used to difficult terrain.

◀ **Rescue dogs must be able to stay focused while searching through rubble.**

▲ **Search and rescue dogs train on rubble piles to toughen their feet.**

Back in the United States, they had practiced walking on rubble piles every week.

Stetson worked quickly. The strong Labrador retriever pulled Olvera forward. Stetson stopped and sniffed the air looking for human scents. Olvera watched his rescue partner closely. Stetson would alert him when he caught a scent.

Soon Stetson moved faster through the rubble, jumping over **obstacles**. He stopped and stuck his nose into a hole. Then he started barking. This was his alert for Olvera. Olvera quickly gathered a bigger rescue team. Had Stetson found a survivor?

▲ Rescue teams from around the world helped search for people after the 2015 Nepal earthquake.

Chapter 2

BECOMING OFFICIAL

Stetson was older than many of the other dogs when he started his search and rescue training. Many SAR dogs begin training as puppies. They must be at least eight weeks old. Police dogs that are already highly trained can join SAR teams, too.

SAR dog handlers look for certain **traits** in dogs. SAR dogs sniff for human scents. They must have a good sense of smell. SAR dogs also learn skills and **commands** throughout their training. It is important for the dogs to be able to learn quickly. Stetson had all the right traits, and so did Hunter.

Hunter was a mixed-breed dog from Kentucky. He got along with other animals. He was also obedient.

◄ **Dogs must pass many obedience tests in order to become search and rescue dogs.**

Hunter was picked for a search and rescue training team. He learned how to pick up scents. His handler hid treats and toys for him to find. When Hunter got better at doing this, the team moved outside. This made it harder for Hunter, since there are more smells outside.

Next Hunter and his handler came up with an alert. An alert lets the handler know when the dog has found a person. An alert can be barking, scratching, digging, or sitting. Once Hunter and his handler felt comfortable with each other, they were ready to become an official team.

Hunter and his handler took a test to join a local SAR organization. There are more than 150 in the United States. Each organization has its own tests to see if a dog and its handler are ready for missions. Hunter and his handler passed the test. They got badges. They could now go on search and rescue missions.

After Hunter and his handler became a team, they went through even more training.

◄ **Search and rescue dogs must learn to get over obstacles.**

Hunter became a **cadaver** dog. He learned how to search for the smell of human remains. He also learned to find drops of blood that people left behind.

Uffda is another SAR dog that works with Hunter. Uffda trained to be a water dog. She rides in a boat along the shore sniffing the water. Uffda helps divers find human scents in the water.

▲ **Water dogs search for human scents that rise up to the surface of the water.**

▲ Avalanche dogs can quickly cover areas that would take humans hours to search on their own.

Lily is an avalanche dog in Canada. She went through extra training, too. She works in the mountains looking for people buried under snow. When she gets a strong scent, she sticks her nose in the snow. If the smell gets stronger, she starts to dig. This is a sign that she has found someone trapped under the snow.

Hunter, Uffda, and Lily are all air scent dogs. They move around looking for where a scent is the strongest. Tank is a trailing dog in Arizona. Tank does not sniff the air. He smells the ground and follows people's footsteps. When people move around, tiny pieces of skin fall off. Tank follows these **particles**.

▲ **Trailing dogs sniff the ground instead of the air.**

▲ Bloodhounds often work as trailing dogs. Bloodhounds have the most sensitive noses of any dog.

Tank's handler keeps him on a long leash. Tank follows the trail wherever it goes. Trailing dogs are great at finding people who have wandered away and become lost.

All types of SAR teams are on call 24 hours a day, year-round. Many SAR dogs live with their handlers. SAR teams must always be ready when a disaster happens.

Chapter 3

MAKING A RESCUE

Stetson continued barking at the pile of rubble. In his training, he learned that when he found a human scent he would get his toy. He wagged his tail excitedly. Soon, the rescue team started to remove the rubble. Stetson and Olvera let the other rescue workers take over.

The workers used machines and shovels to dig down. They worked for six hours. People gathered around to see what would happen. Finally, the workers pulled out a teenage boy. He had been in the rubble for five days between two floors of a collapsed building. The boy was weak but alive. The workers carefully carried him through the crowd. People cheered in celebration.

◄ After hours of digging, workers rescued the boy Stetson had found.

The rescuers took the boy to the hospital. He was scratched and bruised but did not have bad injuries.

Olvera rewarded Stetson with his toy. He had done his job well. His training as an air scent dog had paid off. He had saved another life. Stetson and other SAR dogs around the world help make sure that missing people are found.

THINK ABOUT IT

- Bigger breeds usually make the best search and rescue dogs. Why do you think being bigger is helpful for this job?
- Do you think it is necessary for SAR dogs and their handlers to go through years of training? Why or why not?
- SAR dogs must be friendly and good with people. Why do you think this is an important trait?

◀ **Handlers reward their dogs for jobs well done.**

GLOSSARY

cadaver (kuh-DAV-ur): A cadaver is a dead body. Some search and rescue dogs are trained to find a cadaver.

commands (kuh-MANDS): Commands are orders given by someone. Handlers have specific commands for their dogs.

handlers (HAND-lurs): Handlers are people who train animals. All search and rescue dogs work with handlers.

magnitude (MAG-ni-tood): Magnitude is a number that reflects the power of an earthquake. An earthquake with a higher magnitude does more damage.

obstacles (AHB-stuh-kuhls): Obstacles are things that block a path. Search and rescue dogs must move over or around obstacles.

particles (PAR-ti-kuhls): Particles are very small pieces of something. Some search and rescue dogs follow skin particles to find humans.

rubble (RUHB-uhl): Rubble is the broken pieces of buildings that have fallen. Search and rescue dogs can find people buried under rubble.

traits (TRAYTS): Traits are qualities that make people or animals different from one another. Certain traits make for better search and rescue dogs.

TO LEARN MORE

Books

Goldish, Meish. *K-9 Cops*. New York: Bearport, 2016.

Rudolph, Jessica. *Search-and-Rescue Dogs*. New York: Bearport, 2014.

Zeiger, Jennifer. *Animals Helping After Disasters*. New York: Children's Press, 2015.

Web Sites

Visit our Web site for links about search and rescue dogs: childsworld.com/links

Note to Parents, Teachers, and Librarians: We routinely verify our Web links to make sure they are safe and active sites. So encourage your readers to check them out!

SELECTED BIBLIOGRAPHY

Blumberg, Jess. "A Brief History of the St. Bernard Rescue Dog." *Smithsonian.com*. Smithsonian Institution, 1 Mar. 2016. Web. 30 Jun. 2016.

Holter, Lauren. "Search & Rescue Dogs in Nepal Are Helping Find Survivors Trapped under Debris." *Bustle*. Bustle, 30 Apr. 2015. Web. 30 Jun. 2016.

Layton, Julia. "How Search-and Rescue Dogs Work." *HowStuffWorks.com*. InfoSpace, 16 Dec. 2005. Web. 30 Jun. 2016.

"Search Dog Training." *VSAR.org*. Ohio Valley Search and Rescue, 2016. Web. 30 Jun. 2016.

INDEX

ABOUT THE AUTHOR

Mirella S. Miller is an author and editor of several children's books. She lives in Minnesota with her husband and their dog.